This book is for you. For the way you listen, the love you share, the things you do to brighten my day. It's for all the ways you set a beautiful example of everything it means to be a friend. I think, all the time, how lucky I am to have you in my life.

We laugh at things that no one else would understand.

We've been through so much together,
and still look forward to more.

I don't have to explain myself

You always understand.

We make
great moments
happen without
even trying.

We never run out of goo

mportant things to say.

We know when to
be silly, and when
to be sincere.

When it comes to enthusiasm
and laughter, we don't hold back.

Whatever we do, wherever we go,
our time together is good time.

We want the best
for each other.

We've had our arguments and made our mistakes. But we've never given up on each other.

Even in silence, we understand each other.

You remind me of
what's truly important.

We can count on each other,
even on the darker days.

Everything in our
history makes us look
forward to our future.

Our differences keep things interesting.

Together, we can
simply be ourselves.

We know just how
to challenge each other.

We seek out joy wherever we go.

Your happiness
brings out mine.

We can take on anything together.
And we will.

We listen to each other's deepest hopes, even when they're unspoken.

We help each other
discover our capabilities.
We redefine what's
possible.

Our friendship is full of surprises.

You uplift, support, and encourage me. And I hope to do the same for you.

Time and distance couldn't change what we have. We've made our friendship to last.

We have each other.
Lucky us.

With special thanks to the
entire Compendium family.

Credits:
Written by: M.H. Clark
Design & Illustration by: Jill Labieniec
Edited by: Amelia Riedler
Creative Direction by: Julie Flahiff

ISBN 978-1-935414-84-1

3rd printing. Printed in China with soy inks.